MARC RIBOUD
IN CHINA

Forty years of photography

MARC RIBOUD
IN CHINA

Forty years of photography

Preface by Jean Daniel

THAMES AND HUDSON

To Catherine

"Nothing is more revealing than to compare a country with itself,
while capturing its differences to try to find the thread of its continuity."

Henri Cartier-Bresson

Translated from the French Quarante ans de photographie en Chine *by Ruth Sharman*
Preface by Jean Daniel translated from the French by Aaron Asher

Art Direction and Book Design by Robert Delpire, Idéodis

First Published in Great Britain in 1997 by Thames and Hudson Ltd, London

British Library Cataloguing-in-Publication Data
A catalogue record for this book is available from the British Library

ISBN 0-500-54205-8

Printed and bound in France

Journeys to the Ends of All Chinas

Jean Daniel

A reality for the more than a billion people who live there, China is a myth for the five and a half billion others, registering as such on the world's imagination. If we do not take on the full extent of that imagined China, we cannot call ourselves completely human, members of the human race. This is a remark I heard in Algiers from the philosopher Jean Grenier in my final year of secondary school. He was quoting his friend Etiemble, a historian of comparative literature and an expert on China. For me the idea serves as a call to order whenever, claiming to speak of humanity as a whole, I forget about China. All the more so since, if there are many Chinas in space, there have been only about two Chinas in time. I shall come back to this. What I want to say at the very beginning is that Marc Riboud, without setting out to do so, or presuming to have done it, has created a synthesis of all Chinas.

We willingly speak of China in the singular. Of India too, ever since Pakistan's secession. But for some time that singularity, that expression of oneness, has meant above all that the multiplicity of landscapes and peoples it comprises is based on Maoism's phantom uniformity. It is perhaps also a way of evoking what is called eternal China. But don't go looking for it: what we call 'eternal' is continuity. Eternal France is that of the Ancien Régime and of the Revolution. Eternal Russia is that of Gogol, Pushkin and the tsars as well as of Solzhenitsyn and Stalin. In *The Brothers Karamazov* (Ivan's monologue), one can find in one and the same sentence both the 'Tsar of all the Russias' and the 'God of eternal Russia'. Thus China in its continuity, in the last forty years at any rate, is here restored to us in this striking, disconcerting, now tender and now tragic succession of photographs by a man who knows how to see.

A photographer is a remarkable phenomenon. Looking at the same thing alongside him, we become aware that though we certainly looked, unlike him we did not see. Or at any rate, what we saw was something else. Unless we hold this against the artist, we blame ourselves and are filled with gratitude toward him. For he restores to us what we should have seen. What we should have remembered. What was worth perceiving in the confused panorama of our general vision.

That is why I believe that, whatever the degree of new photographic equipment's automation and sophistication, the famous camera's eye is never independent. It is like a robot before it has been programmed. God knows how many photographs of China I have seen in my life – China old and new, China

the very ancient and the most modern. But I need no more than a few seconds to discern the two contributions without which a photographer is merely an automatic recording device: information and point of view.

Let us dwell on this double definition. Information: photographers like Marc Riboud are driven to it naturally. It is their craft to seize in an instant the trait, attitude, character of a person or situation. If there is a correspondence between a photograph and an event, it is because time has stopped, that is to say has been done away with. Engaging in reflection takes time. In an instant there can only be a reflex. But it is all there. A photographer's reflexes must be educated to prompt him to seize information and prompt the viewer to reflect on or daydream about the reflex's outcome.

Point of view: once the information has been seized and retrieved, highlighting, enhancement, selection can begin – or, as painters do, evaluation of the relationships of volumes and the play of light and shade, close-ups and subtle perspectives. And then we are in the presence of art itself. Why does all that seem more interesting to me now than it did before? Because on this subject we are all more or less still influenced by Roland Barthes, who certainly remains irreplaceable but was writing at a time before the great increase in the technical facility of photographic equipment. When facility to such a degree is not completely mastered, it must be considered an obstacle.

We have now actually reached the point where the automatic taking of photographs is as natural as speaking or writing. But this is precisely the point at which we should remember that we are not speakers or writers simply because we know how to speak or write. In fact, I believe that, far from being enriching for the artist (it is obviously so for the amateur), the perfecting of equipment presents a test. Only to the extent that he masters his technique can he hope to achieve his art.

I indulge myself in this meditation on the art of photography only because I have followed Marc Riboud's route. A hurried amateur (who would quickly have his fill of it) would be content with superficially recording that China is much changed since it went from the puritanical austerity of Maoism to the permissive disorder of the market economy. This collection of photographs, to the contrary, has everything it takes to disconcert, shake and even astonish. The contrasts are skilfully put in relief, as are the contradictions between the beauty of young women's and old people's faces on the one hand, and the squalor of prostitutes and shantytowns on the other.

All of this constitutes unimpeachable reportage. Whether we leaf through this book or linger over it, we are drawn in and then held.

But these, after all, are the emotions we can have in the new Russia or in old Brazil. So we can wonder where in these photographs is China's essence and what in Marc Riboud's art reconstructs it for us. In 1981 I was invited by Claude Martin, then Minister counsellor in Beijing before becoming French ambassador to China, to join a group of artists, writers, and thinkers at a round table for a sumptuous meal. Someone asked me what subject I was most deeply concerned with. Not wanting to embarrass either my host or his guests, I avoided bringing up anything too directly political. I merely said that I wished I were learned enough, and had enough time, to study in depth whether capitalism had disrupted tradition more in Japan than Marxism had in China. That reflection initially prompted everyone to a thoughtful silence and then to endless chatter, especially from the film-makers, who already at that time saw themselves as representing such disruption in their images.

An old man, whose name I have forgotten but who seemed to command a certain authority among the others, spoke up: 'Before comparing the disruptions, you should compare the traditions. In Japan as well as in China – despite what the Japanese say – the man who has dominated our unconscious for more than two thousand years is Confucius; in China, therefore, you should not study the relations between Marxism and tradition but rather the conflict between Mao and Confucius'. He then fell silent. Everyone was silent. Not only out of respect for the wise old man, or out of consideration for the profundity of his remark, but, as I would later learn, because in his later years Mao had affirmed his contempt for Confucius, holding him responsible for all the social and technological backwardness of Chinese society prior to the arrival of the Communists.

I was undoubtedly far from being a Confucius expert and am no more so today. But I did begin to read the texts and the commentaries and finally the assessments. Confucius (or Kong Quiu, 551 – 479 BC) belonged to the highest aristocracy. Although his father was a nobleman and high-ranking official, the family was very poor and Confucius was forced to enter public service in a minor position. He became a kind of specialist of protocol, of proper manners, of respect for customs and the cultivation of rites. Actually, far from being a figure at court, an adviser of courtiers or social arbiter, Confucius devoted himself to the study of the philosophy of the rites, that is of all the traditional and religious ceremonies. Out of that philosophy he built a genuine morality and a real politics. He became a kind of sage, an enlightened conservative, a religious agnostic convinced of his mission to re-establish the social order through the cult of ritual. 'Ritualization' is central to Confucius, and it is precisely what Mao much later reproached him for. According to Léon Vandermeersch, Confucian religion is characterized by two determining factors: the supremacy

of ancestor worship and the major role of divination. The same author quotes a remark by Confucius: 'Without rites, respect is mere satisfaction; without rites, prudence is mere timidity; without rites, frankness is mere arrogance.' When one thinks about it, that remark is amazing. First, because in the monotheistic religions wise men, prophets, reformers have spent their time showing that rites are meaningless without the spirit that animates them and that, if necessary, a man of healthy mind can do very well without them. It is only in traditional religious texts much later than the original revelations that the Talmud, the Church Fathers, and the Hadiths of the Koran transform improvised rites (often borrowed, moreover, from pre-revelation societies) into dogmatic prescriptions. The idea that ceremony, gesture, and staging are almost more important than the rest epitomizes a civilization. When he was reproached for respecting the ritual sacrifice of sheep, Confucius replied: "You love sheep, I love ceremony."

Confucius' text reminds us that before being turned upside down by a market economy (of controlled capitalism, intermittent liberalization of moral standards, an entertainment industry and the infernal cycle of poverty, drugs, crime), Chinese society had already undergone a first great upheaval: that caused by Maoism's egalitarian and standardizing puritanism. The ritualization of everyday life, which, as we saw in the Confucius quotation, had been of extraordinary importance, was utterly changed. One man was raised above a society that had had no notion of transcendence. Hierarchies were abolished in a society that had consisted of class, caste and rank. Uniforms were put on people who had devoted all their imagination to inventiveness in dress and gesture. During the years of the Cultural Revolution, all the roots of patriarchal society were anathematized. The only thing that seemed to have been preserved was the interdiction of sexuality.

Raised by a Confucian father, Mao Tse-tung (or Mao Zedong) grew to be filled with a tenacious hatred for Confucius and took it into his head to liberate the Chinese people from that pernicious philosophy. He accused him of 'being a corrupt culture's perfect and saintly mummified king in whose name the Chinese were forbidden to study science and technology....'

The eruption of peasant Bolshevism into the world's most populous country is a phenomenon as extraordinary, if not more so, as the transfer of Christian authority from Rome to Constantinople. Like the rest of us, Marc Riboud for years has been following the advances and retreats, the disturbances and surprises of that new socialist religion which was a dream for so many people before it became a nightmare for many more. It seemed that the Chinese were searching for something that we too wanted. This, in fact, was the title of a weighty study that caused much ado in France. What were they searching for? Quite simply the realization of a dream so closely linked to man's aspirations that one could call it an innate part of the human spirit. It was the dream of the Amerindians, of the Mesopotamian and

Sumerian sects, of the first Christians, of the famous Paraguay Jesuits, and, more recently, of the Russians, of Vietnam, Cuba, Algeria, of Benin and Cambodia, Guinea and Korea. Do these countries have anything in common? Nothing except egalitarian utopia achieved as authoritarian barbarism. The monstrous dimensions of this barbarism have been sufficiently described, recounted, inventoried to make dwelling on them here unnecessary. Except perhaps to acknowledge the merits of Simon Leys, the earliest of the accusers. On the other hand, no one now under the age of twenty-five can have any idea of the hope, enthusiasm, devotion, the spirit of sacrifice that Maoism could inspire. For what is most strange is that the repentant Maoists are more concerned with denouncing their error and flagellating themselves than with making us understand what it was that attracted them to Maoism. If, before beginning to write, they had taken one last look at certain of Marc Riboud's photographs they would once again have accompanied him on a thoroughly instructive journey. The blindness of foreign Maoists was actually fostered by an immense generosity, a frantic wish to believe in this new man heralded two thousand years before by the Gospel. How many Jesuits and Dominicans have we seen return from China filled with admiration for a country that had become a kind of gigantic monastery rejecting the individualism, egotism and easy comforts of the West? Rather than the failure of an economic system, they claimed to see in China's poverty a virtuous austerity. Mao had indeed eliminated the elite so dear to Confucius. But the true believer, as they saw it, was Mao himself! And when China became a great economic and military power, we remember – we can still hear his voice – that De Gaulle called China 'that civilization older than History itself'.

I bring all this up because Marc Riboud had it in mind in showing us these images; we can see its traces everywhere. What is hard to understand, and harder to imagine, is that the answer to the question I asked the Chinese intellectuals at the French Embassy about Marxism's effect on Chinese tradition would be so surprising. Tradition, I was told, had managed to survive under cover of Marxist modernity. Last year, an official Beijing daily ran the following story. A young man who already owned two companies had signed a contract to manage an affiliated company in the south. The burden of running the affiliate was so great that he asked his father to lend a hand. Thanks to the father's unremunerated efforts, the company generated a 600,000-yuan (about $72,000) profit. The son believed he should thank his father. He thought to use the opportunity of the toasts at a Chinese New Year party to presume to give his father a gift. But with unintentional impudence he covered the gift in a red wrapping – in Chinese tradition exclusively a father's right. To make matters worse, during the course of the celebration the son solemnly declared: 'Father, to compensate you for your trouble, I present you a year-end bonus of 50,000 yuan [$6,000].' His father then exploded with anger. 'Can it be that you consider your father an employee and wish to pay me as such? You are

my son, and that is why I helped you. What a father gives his son cannot be repaid, especially not with money.'

The father here considers his son to have been corrupted by the capitalist system. That much is obvious, but what is less so is that the father is reacting as if he had not lived his entire life under Maoism, as if he were still living in the Confucian time. In a certain sense we might deduce, at least in this instance, that capitalism has more drastically disrupted the son's tradition than Marxism has that of the father. All of this needs nuancing, and it is the nuances that are fascinating. They are what I look for in photographs – scenes, faces, contrasts.

Nowadays, meanwhile, the Beijing newspaper *Renmin Ribao* signals a return in force of traditional thinking: 'Faced with the West's lesson-givers, we are trying to bring about the triumph of past virtues and to correct Mao with Confucius.' While they wait for that, the uprooted, the disoriented, and the film-makers devote themselves to their heart's content to describing a society in hectic change.

Innocent girls, 'gentle and well-bred, turn into restless women rumbling like thunder. People then sigh that the world has lost a girl to gain a lioness.' Simple, innocent little children cherished by their parents become girls who, in school or in work units, are the objects of attention from boys and teachers who are not always protective or disinterested.

Those who are about to take political power in China are already announcing their major concerns. Their hearts and minds tell them that their society will be 'Maoist, Confucian, and nationalist'. They cannot manage in China without Confucius, that mainspring of all that went before, but what does their impulse to brandish nationalism mean? It shows that an initial consequence of the market economy has been the emergence of a society that, no longer egalitarian as it was in Mao's time, no longer traditional as it was in Confucius' time, must now inquire into its own identity. But there are always two kinds of nationalism: one that is proud enough of its values to promote them and another that seeks to excuse all its incapacities with aggression.

As we proceed through Marc Riboud's book, taking in the successive images of disruption caused by progress, a question totally simple in its harshness inevitably arises: we know roughly what China's tradition was, but what then is its modernity? Is it perhaps the nearly spiritual beauty of that young actress? Perhaps it is those young lovers now allowed to sit together on a public bench and that young manager proclaiming his financial successes on wall posters, like the Stakhanovite workers of Shanghai who wore lists of their technical feats on their jackets. Modernity is definitely the nation's prodigious economic expansion and the benefits it certainly brings to, say, a tenth of the population. The spectacle of these anomalies and upheavals is extraordinary. Now is the time for their evaluation, and to our good fortune it is concurrent here with a great photographer's evaluation of his own work.

Translated from the French by Aaron Asher

China in black and white

These photographs are my travel notes. They record more than they analyse or judge. 'The eye', as Walker Evans said, 'traffics in feelings not in thoughts.' It does so even though feelings and thoughts often nourish each other.

If photographs can show us the world, especially as it changes, it is nonetheless difficult to make a portrait of a China that is moving so rapidly. The image is likely to be blurred and even contradictory. In the many streets and villages I strolled through, a glimpse was often refuted by the next one, yesterday's by today's. But going from one world to another stimulates curiosity. Surprises felt by a stroller in China will also, I hope, be felt by viewers of these pages, which, in a play of mirrors and of contrasts, intentionally disregard both chronology and geography.

This is China in black and white. But not everything there is black. Nor is it rose-coloured. Nor is it red: Communism is less talked about in Shanghai than in Paris.

The Chinese like to compare themselves to bamboo, which bends but does not break. I saw them bend under Mao's iron rule when he sought to free them forever from the profit system and from inequality. Nowadays we see them riding on a new wave of money-making, commerce, speculation, activities in which they have always excelled. This surge of modernism, originating in Taiwan and Hong Kong, simultaneously awakened the old beliefs outlawed by Mao. Is it fair to say, then, that in China everything moves and nothing changes? That Maoism was only a parenthesis?

These extremely gifted capitalists have created a prodigious economic boom that fascinates our world and has enabled innumerable Chinese to scale the sacred mountain of consumerism. At the same time, the beauties of an ancient culture seem to be fading before our eyes. But do we have the right to be saddened by this when no one in China, even those who are being left behind economically, wishes to return to the Mao years? And yet the East that we loved for its permanences is suddenly turning into a caricature of the West, in a race that is probably an accelerated version of ours.

As a young engineer, I was fascinated by the symmetry of pendulum swings. I witnessed the most spectacular of such swings in China when a billion monks and nuns broke out of their monasteries and convents and, sowing their wild oats, launched themselves toward the paradise of the dollar and of licentiousness. Does the great width of the swing of Chinese society prefigure a new and equally strong return swing?

Marc Riboud

The photographs are organized into three chapters:

1

Old China as I saw it on the occasion of my earliest visits.

2

Old China and new China and China under Mao, in a series of juxtaposed images.

3

Radical images of new China and the economic boom.

The captions together with my personal notes appear at the end of the book. The names of towns, provinces and individuals appear alongside the photographs in the transliteration system that has now been adopted worldwide (Pinyin). These forms are also used in the text and captions, with the old forms given in parentheses on their first appearance. The only exception is Canton, which has been so called in the captions (though not alongside the pictures) since the new form, Guangzhou, is still unfamiliar in English.

1

1957
Sichuan

1985
Huang-Shan

1965
Guangxi

1957

Beijing

1957
Beijing

1965

Beida

1957

Beijing

779

A0017183

1965

Liulichang

1957

Shaanxi

1957
Anshan

1957
Beijing

1957

Beijing

1957
Anshan

1971
Shaanxi

1957

Hebei

1957
Yangtze

1957

Wuhan

1957
Sichuan

1957
Anshan

1957
Beijing

2

1957
Mao Zedong

1971
Shanghai

1957

Yanan

1965
Tiananmen

1957

Shanghai

1995
Taiyuan

1971
Wuhan

1994
Beijing

49

1957

Beijing

1992

Shanghai

1965

Beijing

1992

Shanghai

1965
Shenyang

1957

Beijing

1995

Shanghai

1957
Shaanxi

1992

Shenzhen

1957

Beijing

1992
Shanghai

1965

Guangzhou

1992
Shanghai

1957

Beijing

1992
Shanghai

1957
Beijing

1992

Beijing

1965

Shanxi

1993

Gong Li

1957
Beijing

1993
Shanghai

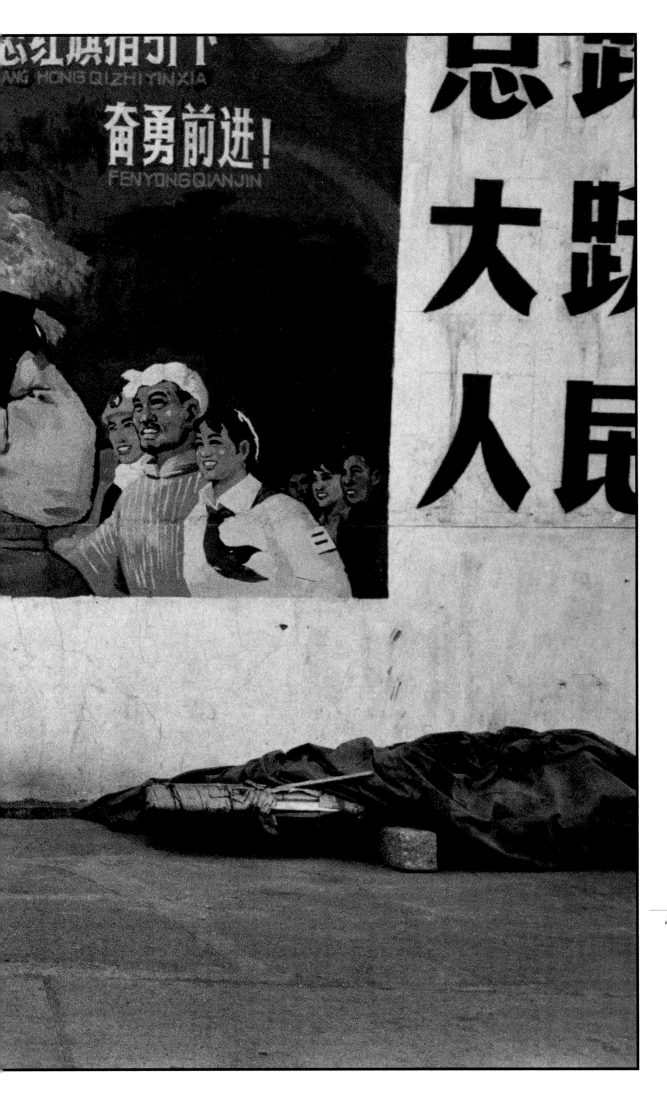

1965

Shanghai

1971
Beijing

1993
Shanghai

1965

Beijing

1995
Hunan

1957

Beida

1994
Beijing

1957
Beijing

1995
Taiyuan

1957

Hunan

1995

Zhejiang

1957

Shaanxi

1993
Shanghai

1956
Guangzhou

1995

Shanghai

1965

Hohhot

1992
Tiananmen

1957

Hebei

1993
Shanghai

1971

Hebei

1995

Shanghai

1965
Guangxi

1993

Shenzhen

1965

Guangxi

1995
Taiyuan

1957

Beijing

1985
Hefei

1957

Beijing

1993
Shenzhen

1957

Shenyang

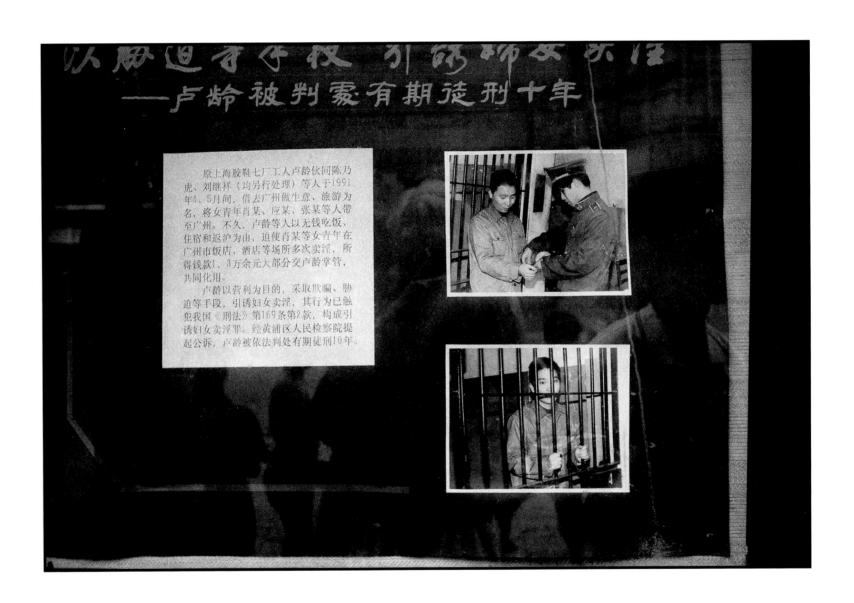

1992

Shanghai

1965

Beijing

1982

*Deng
Xiaoping*

1971

Zhou Enlai

1995

Taiyuan

1993

Shenzhen

3

1993
Tiananmen

1993
Shenzhen

112

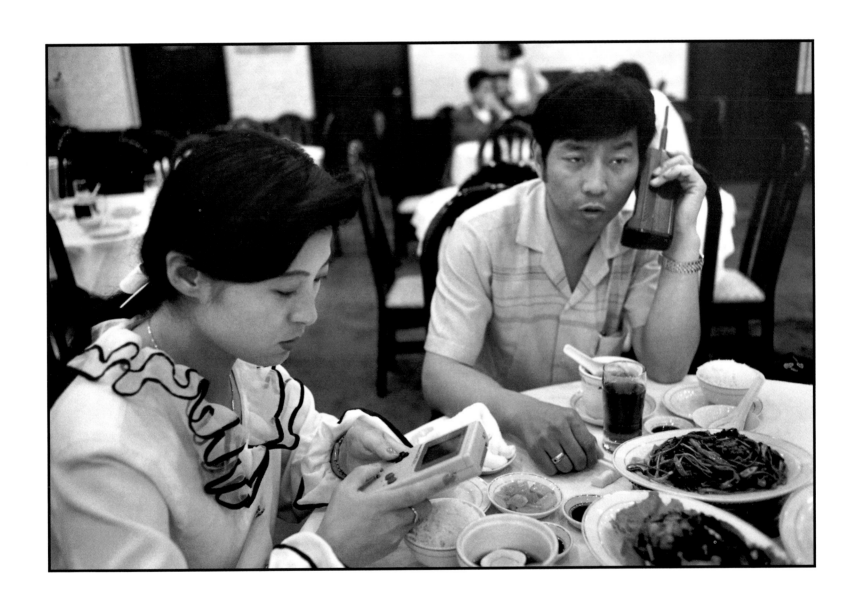

1993

Guangzhou

1993

Shandong

1992
Beijing

1993
Shanghai

1993

Beijing

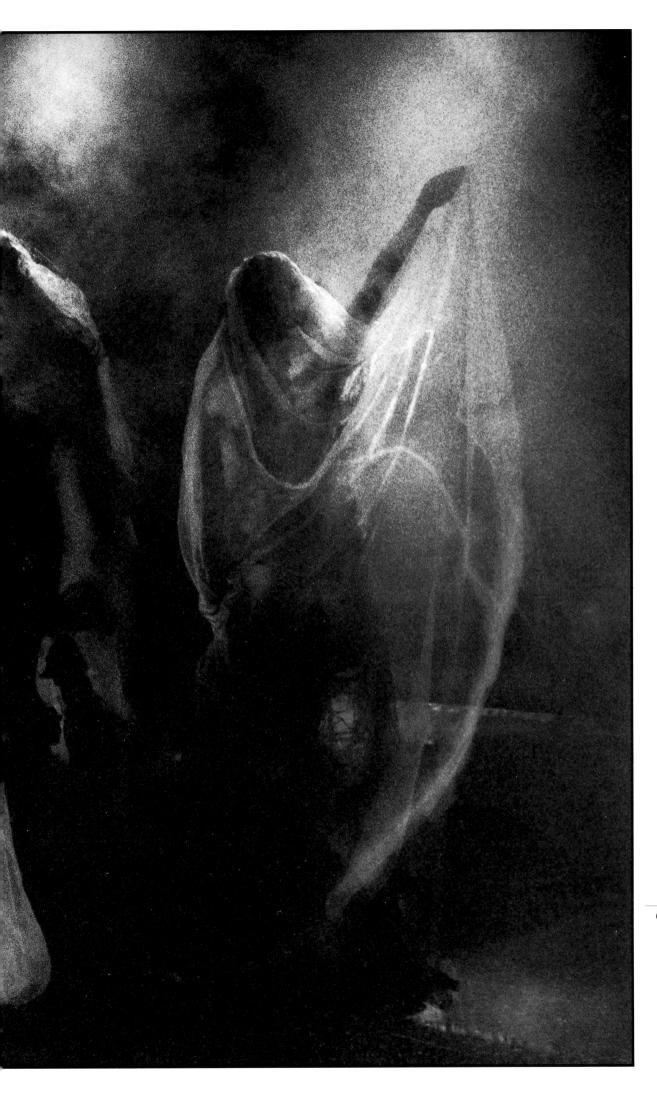

1992
Guangzhou

1992

Beijing

1992

Shenzhen

1993
Shanghai

1993
Shanghai

1993

Shenzhen

1984
Beijing

1992

Shanghai

1993

Beijing

1993

Shenzhen

1993

Shanghai

1993

Beijing

1992

Shenzhen

1992
Beijing

135

1995

Shanghai

1995

Taiyuan

1993
Shenzhen

1995
Taiyuan

1993

Beijing

1995

Shanghai

1995
Zhejiang

1992
Shenzhen

1992
Shenzhen

1993

Shanghai

1993

Shanghai

1993

Shanghai

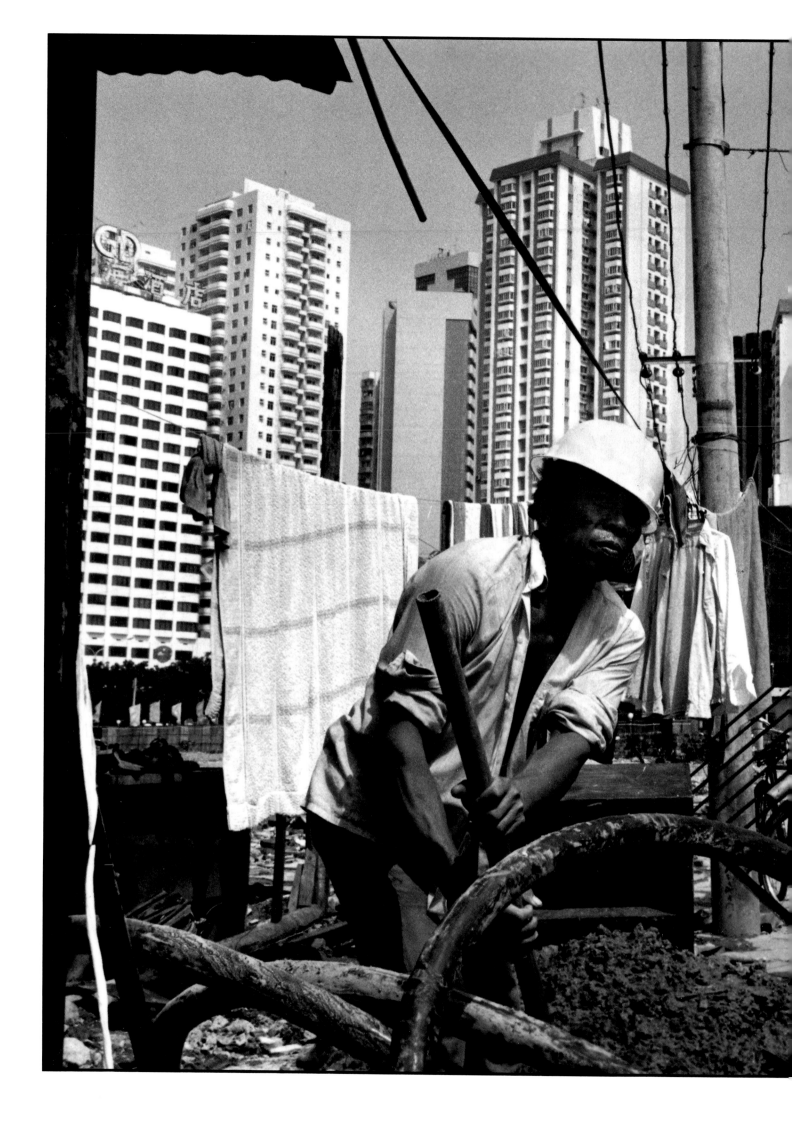

1993
Shenzhen

1992

Guangzhou

1992
Shenzhen

153

1993

Shanghai

1995
Taiyuan

1993

Shenzhen

1993

Shenzhen

1994
Beijing

1994

Dalian

1994

Dalian

1992

Shenzhen

1994

Shenzhen

1994

Shenzhen

1992

Shanghai

Forty years of photography in China

I have travelled through much of northern and southern China on foot, often alone, often accompanied by a 'guardian angel' – though by walking faster than they did I could sometimes shake them off. My Chinese guides never imposed any restrictions: they would simply say 'It is time to go home' and I would do my best to prevent them losing face. In 1957 Sichuan was the most Chinese of China's provinces, the most fertile and densely populated; the most backward too, since it was also the most isolated.

12-13

The origins of Chinese art lie here, and as I climbed those several thousand steps carved into the rock, I understood why. This mountain has inspired artists and poets and cannot fail to inspire the photographer too. I love mist and shadows, as I love the moment when night begins to fall, and thanks to such effects one gets a clearer sense here of depth and perspective than in other places. The wind sweeps the clouds across, creating rhythms and rhymes. The mountain is a place of poetry, music and painting, and the guardian angels like the apparatchiks remain down below.

14

It rains a great deal in the southern part of China – ideal conditions for the rice, the staple food crop here. In 1965 these schoolchildren are still wearing the hats worn by their grandfathers as protection against the rain, though the younger ones can scarcely cope with the size. One or two hats per family would be passed on from one generation to the next.

15

In 1957 Beijing (Peking) was no more than a large village criss-crossed with alleyways of beaten earth known as *hutong*. The inhabitants were forbidden to build their houses higher than the walls of the Forbidden City – and who would dare to aspire higher than the Emperor himself? Such building restrictions made the old city a pleasing place which concrete monstrosities have since disfigured. Among the sounds of the city minor tradesmen such as glaziers, grinders and tinkers each create a distinctive melody of their own. The coal merchant here sells a coarse dust which is baked into small lumps in the family mould. The dragons decorating the edge of the roof mark this out as a royal dwelling; their purpose is to ward off evil spirits.

16-17

The winter of 1957 was a particularly bitter one in Beijing. The ground was frozen solid; temperatures dropped to -20 C, and wind whipped up flurries of snow. The streets were empty – except for me and the odd rickshaw minus tyres, pathetically held together with bits of string and carrying a poor little bundle of firewood. My guardian angel, for his part, had long since disappeared, taking refuge in the warmth.

18

Beida, Beijing's university, is famous for its high incidence of student unrest. When I went there in 1965 my guardian angel kept me under particularly close surveillance, electing to restrict my visit to those dormitories whose inmates knew neither French nor English. I was given permission to take photographs as long as I avoided anything that could be regarded as irregular or as evidence of a persistent bourgeois mentality – an old oiled umbrella, for example, or a box of food sent by the student's family. Fortunately my guide was unfamiliar with the tricks of the wide-angle lens. I refrained from pointing out to him and his friends that this girl with her long plaits and her well-pressed trousers, engaged in the individualistic pastime of knitting a jumper for herself, is hardly the epitome of the revolutionary. The mosquito net, however, gets a tick, having received Mao's stamp of approval.

19

An early assembly line: in this workshop making radio sets in Beijing in 1957 the men and women – working with the same dexterity as the student in the previous photograph – are 'knitting' small splices and gathering them into scraps of newspaper (*The People's Daily* coming in useful here).

20-21

Some free time for shopping: unaccompanied by my guardian angel, I venture into the Antique Dealers' Street in Liulichang; but two young girls have spotted me and are watching my every move, as if they had assumed the role of voluntary guardians. These windows are typically Chinese, dividing the street into a series of tableaux. The notice in the shop window to the left says 'Diamonds, pearls, jade and china bought'. In 1965 there were food shortages in Beijing and the inhabitants had to resort to selling their family heirlooms for the equivalent of a few pence. It would have been quite unacceptable to wear them. A year later, under the Cultural Revolution, people were forced to give all their gold and jewelry to the State, receiving nothing in exchange: failure to do so would have incurred public shame or worse.

22

Wheat, noodles and steamed, stuffed bread are the staples of the northern Chinese diet. Spaghetti was not an invention of the Italians but was introduced to the Venetians by Marco Polo, who took some to Italy in his luggage. Here in Shaanxi, in 1957, collective farming was compulsorily introduced by the people's communes. The collapse of the communes in the sixties led to food shortages and even famine. At that time *The People's Daily* advised against running 'so as to conserve energy' and several million deaths were attributed to 'natural disasters'.

23

My guardian angel was delighted to be able to vaunt China's achievements since the Liberation (Mao's seizure of power in 1949) and was always talking about 'before' and 'after'. '*Before* men used to go about in bare feet here and the rope would cut into their shoulders. *Afterwards* they were entitled to wear sandals and softer strips of material on their shoulders.' In 1957, however, pulling a boat against the Yangtze's current below Chongqing still required a monumental effort that made men into beasts of burden.

24-25

The abacus is a Chinese invention and has still not been completely super-seded by the pocket calculators imported from Japan – even where dollars are being reckoned in millions. In 1957 this steelworks engineer in Manchuria has a different telephone for every line. Switchboards were not introduced until fifteen years later.

26

Roaming round old Beijing, unhampered by guardian angels, I met with a number of surprises and learnt a great deal about China as it used to be. One might wonder, for example, why this apparent torture scene should be offered as entertainment to children. It was on this occasion that I was to learn what the *qigong* signifies. While the 'torturer' puts all his energy into striking his victim (or accomplice), the latter resists the impact of the sledgehammer on the stone by following a principle common to the martial arts and concentrating his breath in his lower abdomen (the area of the body known as *dan tian* or the 'alchemical furnace'). On occasion I have seen the stone smashed to smithereens and the accomplice stand up immediately.

27

In 1957 in the course of my wanderings I also went to the Sky Bridge, the popular artists' quarter in the south of old Beijing, where wrestlers, acrobats, tumblers and puppeteers used to provide a lively source of entertainment on weekdays and particularly Sundays (see the film by Chris Marker). This medley of popular culture rooted in the history of the world's oldest capital city was soon to disappear under the onslaught of Maoist prohibitions. And yet these street displays afforded precious moments of pleasure to old and young alike. What remained of this street culture was finally routed by the introduction of cinema and television and the games imported from the south.

28-29

In 1957 in the canteen at the great steelworks at Anshan in Manchuria (the North East, to be politically correct) workmen and engineers are seated at the same table and, according to Revolutionary practice, wearing the same Mao caps with the same spectacles, eating their bowls of rice with the same chopsticks. Their one privilege was to be able to eat sitting down. Other canteens for workers and students provided no seating accommodation at all.

30

China is like anywhere else: the warmest welcome comes from the poorest quarter. This peasant from Shaanxi, photographed in 1971, almost certainly owns only one shirt to go with his Chinese belt, but his smile is both hospitable and shrewd. Though he has probably lived through years of famine he is clearly proud of the new brick facing to his pisé wall. My guardian angel declined to translate his words of welcome.

31

The Peking Opera was finally crushed under the repeated hammer blows of Mao's single-track philosophy, but in this northern village in 1957 I saw its last few flutters of life. The children were enthralled by the company's acrobatics and sabre games. By opening its doors to the outside world, China is now being flooded with cartoons from Japan that are characterized by a very different kind of violence.

32-33

To see the real China, you need only walk beside the Yangtze, and in 1957 that was even truer than it is today. Everything reflected the old China – the patched sails and junks made of sticks of bamboo lashed together, so that one wondered how they could possibly float; and then those poles – the enduring image of China – carried across the shoulders and involving a careful balancing act which Michaux refers to when he describes: 'On one side an enormous cooking pot singing to itself or a smoking stove, and on the other side boxes and plates or a sleepy child'.

34

The use of patchwork in China is not an aesthetic tradition with any kind of folkloric or ecological basis, and yet this sail seems to stand for the pride of generations who have patched, tied, darned and mended and are absolutely indifferent to the bridge being built of Soviet concrete – the first to span the Yangtze.

35

Located in a village in Sichuan, this disused temple was converted into a school by Mao in 1957. Decorated roofs on the right date from the Ming Dynasty and at the back of the courtyard the outline of a tree creates a design resembling Chinese lettering.

36-37

Manchuria passed back and forth between the Russians, the Japanese and Chinese (as well as enduring a number of Western invasions) before becoming part of the People's Republic of China in 1949, along with its enormous mining resources and its dilapidated steelworks. In 1957 the Chinese had begun introducing their own kind of disorder into the region and the first directive from Beijing stated that the name Manchuria was to be replaced by 'North Eastern Province'. The region is rich in coal, and has a corresponding problem with pollution – both being sources of pride in a country that is in the process of building up its heavy industries.

38

Without a guardian angel to accompany me I got lost so often in Beijing that I now know my way round it better than I know certain parts of Paris. These little girls are from poor families (but well wrapped up against the cold) and have probably not started attending school yet. They present a wonderful picture of solidarity in contrast to so many images of modern-day China.

41

In the winter of 1957 I was one of six hundred guests invited to a dinner attended by Mao Zedong (Mao Tse-tung) in Beijing. The dinner was held in the banqueting hall at the former Hôtel des Wagons-Lits Cook, whose silverware was now on sale in a State-run shop in the old town. Among the guests were a handful of heroes from the Long March, all busy imitating Mao and wielding their knives and forks with great aplomb. The only foreign photographer present, I was subject to one mysterious restriction: I was forbidden ever to photograph the Great Helmsman from the front. On this particular evening, however, I managed something of a scoop: Mao, full frontal, drinking a glass of Mao Tai.

42

The austere measures enforced by the Great Cultural Revolution have done nothing to detract from the delicately feminine beauty of this young student at the Shanghai Ballet School, seen here in 1971. According to the rules, the Little Red Book was the only acceptable reading material and Mao's badge the only acceptable jewelry; plaits had to be worn short (and Chinese hair was used to boost the wig trade in the West); and no one could have a sexual relationship before marriage nor marry before the age of 25.

43

It was at Yanan, the destination of the Long March, that Mao Zedong began to elaborate the philosophy that would shape a new China. The monkish cell, the square bed and neatly spread mosquito net, and a cold shower on rising, were tokens of a new life style for which Mao was the first to set the example. In France, in July 1971, Alain Peyrefitte regretted the fact that the French Maoists, with whose lack of discipline he had to deal in May 1968, had failed to learn from the example of their Chinese brothers. Today the Chinese seem to be rapidly regaining their natural tendency to disorderliness – a tendency which, some people say, accounts for their developing such powers of memory and intelligence.

44-45

In 1965 the enemy was America. While the fighting in Vietnam was at its most intense I was in Tiananmen Square one day, standing on the little platform reserved for traffic wardens, while all around me wave after wave of abuse broke as demonstrators hurled insults at the Americans. Day and night, according to *The People's Daily*, more than a million and a half demonstrators marched through the centre of Beijing. Here the long noses, ties and suits, the Uncle Sam hat and the captured airman's jacket symbolize the Western aggressor. It would not be long before other crowds would congregate here and see other movements more spontaneous than this.

46

These crowds are flowing like a tranquil river through the streets of old Shanghai. In 1957 Mao caps were already an obligatory part of male dress. One courageous exception – a white straw hat – creates a little of the atmosphere of the 'Shanghai Triad' dear to Zhang Yimou. The banner in the background carries the injunction 'Avoid the habit of spitting on the ground'. In the centre of the picture a man is managing to slip through the crowd with his balancing pole over his shoulder.

47

One of the consequences of China's sudden switch to a market economy was to promote advertising – and that meant advertising by whatever means possible. Here, in Taiyuan in 1955, under the impassive gaze of an old Ming lion, an enormous inflatable doll wearing a Western-style jacket and tie carries a deliberately ambiguous inscription: 'CARDIN-ER Western clothes'. By adding the ideogram (ER) to a famous designer label popular in China, a clever manufacturer has set out to attract passers-by without laying himself open to accusations of plagiarism. There are those in China who maintain, in any case, that imitation is a sign of homage; but imitation can merge into forgery.

48

At Wuhan, a major industrial centre on the Yangtze, the smoke from these chimneys is blowing in the direction of Mao's lifted arm as if in response to his directive. In 1971 the personality cult of Mao was at its height and artists of varying abilities were invited to contribute to it. If the statue's arm seems out of proportion to the rest of the body, this may have been a way of emphasizing the direction in which to go.

49

On Wangfujing, Beijing's main shopping street, a plastic Superman complete with red cape, a symbol of the West, stands among an array of advertising slogans: 'Computer-tested eyesight … Rapid repairs to watches, Japanese and Swiss cameras … Treatment for yellow teeth …'

50

At the School of Fine Arts in Beijing in 1957 Mao was the students' primary model, followed by the peasant, the worker and the soldier. Since he cannot work from life, this student is using Mao's official portrait and a series of small photos of the great leader taken from different angles and carefully arranged around the official one.

51

The hoardings along the Nanjing Road in Shanghai used at one time to honour the efforts of workers and peasants. Now it is the successes of the new managers which are displayed for public edification. This new company director dressed in Western style is being congratulated for having brought domestic gas to 183,000 homes in Shanghai (which has a population of 13 million).

52

In 1965 China was supporting Vietnam in its struggle against American imperialism. Here we see the two leaders, Mao Zedong and Ho Chi Minh, president of North Vietnam. Fifteen years later China and Vietnam were themselves at war. The slogans were chanted by the party leaders – in this case members of the Institute of Fine Arts – before being repeated by the hordes of demonstrators.

53

In 1992 I visited the Stock Exchange, which had just opened in Shanghai. A speculator, raising his arm in the vigorous gesture of a Maoist militant, is brandishing the journal *The Stock Exchange* (which has a print run of 300,000 and appears on a Monday). An interview with a 'parvenu' (as the paper describes him) is entitled 'Wealth brings with it the need for virtue'. Another nouveau riche tells how 'At one time I was penniless and worked simply to stay alive; now that I have money I am a man – a free man.' The speculators assumed that the market could only continue to rise; when it collapsed the press reported a number of suicides. An old woman with tiny feet came to the counter one day, saying: 'Now the good old days are back, I've brought in my Kuomintang shares.' One wonders if she was any luckier than the holders of Russian imperial bonds.

54-55

In Manchuria in 1965 these hard-faced young pioneers with their wooden rifles made me shudder. And yet we did not know that we were dealing here with the Cultural Revolution's future Red Guards – that they would soon be trading in their wooden rifles for the real thing. It was in the rural areas that the most violent manifestations of the Cultural Revolution occurred. Travelling for free by train, the young Red Guards went about the countryside sowing the seeds of 'revolution within revolution'.

56

In 1957 it was in the Sky Bridge quarter of old Beijing (see photo page 27), where I often wandered about on my own among the troupes of entertainers, that I discovered the best popular circus acts. Such amusements were branded as decadent by the Party line and were soon to disappear. An official State circus training school took their place.

57

These children, like many one sees today in Shanghai's streets, are miming scenes from films imported from Japan and Hong Kong. But they are laughing and this time I feel no cause for concern.

58

Education was one of the success stories of the Maoist regime. In order to institute the new disciplinary measures teachers, like this one, may have relied in part on existing Confucian traditions. The rules were simple and based on ideas like controlling one's emotions and respecting the natural order of things.

59

In Shenzhen in 1992 Mao's image no longer monopolized posters and advertising space, and national newspapers and magazines had begun to compete with Hong Kong's. A pin-up on the cover of a weekly magazine announces the 'major property deal' of a multi-millionaire 'parvenu' who spent £30,000 in the course of a single evening. The press is free to discuss the economy, finance, famous actresses and sex (in so far as Eastern modesty on the subject allows). The slightest criticism of a politician or of a Party decision, on the other hand, is quite unthinkable. There is little place for censure: self-censure is sufficient.

60

The Chinese are a practical people. They invented the wheelbarrow, and even a wheelbarrow that can go up steps and a wheelbarrow equipped with sails. They also invented printing, Indian ink, gunpowder and the rocket. But the most beautiful and the most gratuitous of Chinese inventions is the kite, an object that in China is too delicate to be entrusted to a child. In Tiananmen Square, where it is almost always windy, it is better to look, not at the ground, which still carries the marks of recent events, but at the sky and the spectacle that is for ever unfolding there – dragons tens of feet long wheeling and spiralling to make shapes as graceful and as complex as Chinese letters.

61

The Chinese may not have invented advertising – a manifestation of capitalist corruption according to the Maoist way of thinking – but they soon made very good use of it and massive painted hoardings appeared on the walls of towns and even villages, the scale of such advertising sometimes exceeding anything to be found in the West. This black and white advertisement on a wall in Shanghai in 1992 reads: 'Today you are 20; in a year's time you will be 18 thanks to our beauty milk.'

62

In 1965, on the eve of the Cultural Revolution, all the films that were released had a propagandist slant. It is unusual to see a Chinese person wandering around town on their own like this stern-faced man, whose expression matches the look on the faces in the poster.

63

Life in China is regulated by customs, southern customs being the most fashionable. These customs relate, on the one hand, to ancient beliefs (often wrongly described as 'superstitions') and, on the other, to such things as décor: in particular the use of mirrors to cover the interior walls of large shops, thereby multiplying the numbers of consumers. They even have a bearing on the escalators that link the many levels of these sacred mountains of consumerism and form part of the layout of large shops like the Galeries Lafayette, Printemps and Carrefour. Taiwanese and Hong Kong influences contribute a flashy, colourful element but also a return to the geomancy abolished by Mao.

64

My guardian angel found two things to be proud of in this scene, taken in 1957 in the suburbs of Beijing: the smoke, a sign of modernization, and the newly built pagoda, intended not as a place of worship but to disguise a reservoir.

65

Shanghai, 1992: these people's homes have been destroyed to make way for new tower blocks. They wait to be rehoused, living meanwhile in shanty towns among piles of household appliances, fans, fridges and televisions.

66

Until the age of 4 or 5 children in the country wear trousers split at the crotch. This ancient and most practical of Chinese customs, while circumventing the need for nappies, also seems to make young children aware of hygiene at an earlier age.

67

In this same palace, where the children's trousers are always split, one also sees a motley collection of strange umbrellas today. While the design of this one is totally untraditional, it still serves a function as old as the palace itself: women of good birth in China have always sought to protect their light complexion and the delicate texture of their skin by shading themselves from the sun.

68

The cap was only a small part of Mao's legacy, but by creating his own style of headgear (more than a billion were manufactured) Mao must have been the envy of any fashion designer. This worker at a people's commune in Shanxi is reading the Chinese Youth newspaper. Of the 25,000 or more characters in the Chinese alphabet, the paper uses a total of 2,000. My guardian angel proudly translated for me the headline 'China explodes its second atom bomb'.

69

Gong Li, seen here in her native province, Shandong, while shooting the film *Living*, is the superstar of the Chinese film world, but has held out against the attentions of Hollywood. Adopting a Western style that is simpler but also more brilliant and more brightly coloured, Gong Li embodies the Chinese ideal of femininity. She has thrown off a number of taboos but still remains close to her peasant grandmother.

70

I have walked up Wangfujing Street in Beijing more often than I have walked up the Champs-Elysées. Up until the beginning of the 1980s there was nothing very surprising in the sight of those 'blue ants', described by Robert Guillain, passing by on felt-slippered feet. But this woman in her black cape with white fox fur at the neck, smoking a cigarette (formerly the privilege of older women in public) and looking haughtily around at the proletarian crowds, *was* an unusual sight in 1957. Has this aristocrat succeeded in surviving the levelling effects of Maoism?

71

By contrast there is nothing out of the ordinary about this girl, seen in a Shanghai street in 1993. With her 12-speed bicycle made in China, her tiny shorts and the pre-1940s frills on her blouse, she is one of today's typical young Shanghaians, and her confident stride suggests a life largely free from mental problems.

72-73

The Maoist philosophy of the sixties was simple: it was the duty of the worker, the peasant and the soldier to continue to move towards the left in the footsteps of the Great Helmsman. In Shanghai in 1965, while I was preparing to photograph this popular image of the Revolution, my guardian angel asked the sneering docker who was standing in front to move away so as not to tarnish the picture. As he scurried off to the right the man provided the perfect image of a 'rightist' counterrevolutionary!

74

In 1971 Mao was still encouraging people to have large families – maximizing a couple's chances of conceiving a son (the ambition of every Chinese parent) and China's chances of boosting its population figures beyond the billion mark.

75

On this wall in Shanghai in 1993 portraits of Elvis Presley and Chairman Mao hang alongside those of a grandfather and grandmother. In China attitudes to age have remained unchanged: the older a person is the more he is respected and honoured. On the steps of Huang Shan, an old painter, wishing to flatter me, said that I must surely be 'at least 80'!

76

My Maoist years regularly involved lengthy tea-drinking sessions while we listened to soothing speeches under the eyes of Marx, Engels, Lenin and Stalin… Today the images and badges of those great heroes, the historic figureheads of socialism, have ended up on the pavements at flea markets – a sorry conclusion to the revolutionary myths they promoted…

77

Hunan, 1995: this peasant woman is posing in front of a photograph of her dead husband, which hangs next to the one of Chairman Mao. The New Year greetings on the right express the traditional sentiments: 'May good fortune and the message of the gods come to you', 'Be rich and happy'. Immediately to the left of this card hangs a talisman for warding off evil spirits and natural disasters. The presence of Mao's portrait in the group is not, I am told, a proof of political allegiance, but a sign that the old statesman has joined the pantheon of the gods and that he is no longer a wandering soul like some other ancestors. For this peasant woman he has become in a sense the god of the soil and of the harvest.

78

Beida, 1957: at Beijing's university the Saturday evening dance was a hangover of Western bourgeois habits that was soon to be abolished under the party's iron rule. The dancer's mask is intended as a protection against germs and the cold rather than her partner's unwanted kisses.

79

In a five-star hotel in Beijing in 1994 Chinese and Japanese industrialists discuss business while an ancient figure gazes down on the proceedings. Large hotels often decorate their rooms with paintings and sculptures, mostly copies of antique works.

80

In old Beijing in 1957 a banner announces a 'Xiang Sheng' production, a show involving storytellers and clappers. The feather duster (in the foreground) is the most widely used piece of equipment in China. The feathers all have birds' names.

81

Taiyuan, 1995: a family is still living in this old house furnished in the traditional style. They will soon be rehoused in a council flat and their childhood home will be demolished.

82

Hunan province, 1957: this household has probably never seen a 'long nose', the term the Chinese use for a European.

83

A new generation of peasants now lives in the vicinity of Shanghai. The land still belongs to the State, but today families can profit individually from the land they cultivate. This has inspired a degree of motivation that has led to surplus rice production in some provinces such as Anhui, where famine was rife in the sixties.

84

Shaanxi, 1957: these illiterate peasants are attending an evening class, working at tables where young students sit during the day while they are out in the fields. The patched and padded jackets, worn for warmth in the bitter northern winter, are passed down from generation to generation and the Mao cap is the only sign of the changing times.

85

These young women are working for Alcatel, having left the countryside and settled in Shanghai a few years earlier. A Belgian engineer expressed his surprise to me at how swiftly they had adapted to computerized methods of data processing.

86

This was my first Chinese photograph, taken at the end of 1956 during a train journey which took me from the borders of Hong Kong to Canton (Guangzhou), in other words from one world to another. The woman dressed in black is a peasant to judge by her luggage, though from her natural elegance one might imagine her to be a city dweller. The image immediately became superimposed on other remembered images of people utterly abandoned, with not a shred of dignity left to them, that meet one's eyes so often in other parts of Asia. It was this that first impressed me, like other visitors to China, with a sense of the dignity which Mao seemed to have instilled in the Chinese people.

87

Edgar Snow described Shanghai in the forties, a Shanghai that was disappearing with the Revolution, as 'the most disturbing and the most picturesque city in the old Orient'. A new page has been turned and the vices described by Snow are for the most part making a rapid come-back. And if in 1995 stuffed bread is still steamed in wooden sieves in the traditional manner, the advertisement for panties bearing the label 'Three stacked rifles' does a great deal to undermine the sense of modesty which, together with politeness, fidelity and honesty, was one of the four traditional Chinese virtues.

88

Family values and morality have suffered under the onslaught of modernism and financial greed. Such values have survived better in the countryside and there is a clear bond of affection between this herdsman and his son, photographed in the Mongolian steppes in 1965.

89

One of the innumerable amateur photographers in Tiananmen Square in 1992 uses a flagpole to get shade. Country folk come in droves to be photographed at the foot of the banner with the five stars. There is little to remind one here of the events of June 1989. And yet the tanks that entered this square to the dumb astonishment of an entire city have left their mark, pitting the surface of the asphalt, and tens of thousands of drivers passing through here each day must feel the tiny jolts – just sufficient to keep the memory alive.

90

This solemn photograph taken on the Great Wall in 1957 will no doubt occupy a place of honour in the homes of each of these soldiers of the People's Liberation Army. Their children are proud of it, but will their grandchildren be too? The Great Wall was built by the emperor Qin to defend the Empire against barbarian invasion, but today's invaders are the 'Chinese minorities' according to the official, politically correct term.

91

The longest bridge in Asia links Shanghai and Pudong, Asia's future financial capital, which sees itself as a successor to Hong Kong. The name of the bridge, Yangpu, is carved into the concrete in Deng script. My son Alexis is standing at the centre of the bridge.

92

Jogging along the Great Wall was not yet fashionable in 1971, though photography was beginning to be. In the background, almost lost in the mist, a group of French government officials, come to evaluate the risks of China's political reawakening, are gathered around a former minister. A walk along the Great Wall is a favourite Sunday pastime, popular with tourists and local people alike.

93

Multi-level interchanges like this one in Shanghai, photographed in 1995, will perhaps prove to be the cathedrals of Chinese cities at the end of our century. Looming large in the landscape, these vaulted concrete structures with their massive pillars are the pride of modern China and the car has become at last an integral part of Chinese civilization. Today Beijing, with its million cars and eight million bicycles, is in the process of building its third ring road.

94

Chinese patchwork is the product of necessity. A patched jacket can serve several generations of a family, but whoever sewed this one ran out of thread. At the start of the Cultural Revolution peasants, soldiers and intellectuals were 'forced' to work together at this construction site, and so that they would never forget them, the words 'The Party Line' were painted on the side of the dyke which they were building.

95

At this construction site in Shenzhen, in 1993, the work is less arduous and workmen are required to wear helmets. The splendour of these tower blocks is a function of glass, concrete and glazed tiles rather than architectural rigour. When I arrived in China for the first time in 1957 Shenzhen was no more than a fishing village. Today three million people from throughout China have converged on Shenzhen and are building a city fit to rival Hong Kong. In 1997 Hong Kong will become part of China again, but in the meantime China is doing its utmost to catch up with Hong Kong. Which, one wonders, will contaminate the other?

96

Guangxi province, 1965: the man on the right carrying the balancing pole is a medical student, as his T-shirt reveals; the man in glasses on the left could be a philosophy teacher. These people are building a road. An entire generation of students was forced under Mao to undertake the most strenuous manual work. That generation has been sacrificed: today most are unemployed or have become social drop-outs.

97

In 1995 I discovered that I was able to travel increasingly freely throughout China. One day my friend Liu and I found ourselves 200km from Taiyuan, in the heart of China's richest coal-mining country. The mine we were visiting was much as I imagine mines to have been in 19th-century Britain, the only tools being a pick and shovel. We took pictures and the miners smiled for the camera (the boss rather less), and at the end of the day we were arrested for industrial espionage. We were interrogated for hours on end by a series of different interrogators, who were rather less forthcoming with their smiles than the miners had been. Behind us an impressive-looking machine gun was pointing, reassuringly, in the other direction – reassuringly, that is, until my friend Liu whispered to me: 'It swivels!' The policemen threatened to confiscate our passports, cameras and films. By late evening we parted company from them, almost friends after both sides had succeeded in saving face. In China the art of saving face allows one to extricate oneself from a number of sticky situations.

98

Modesty is one of the oldest Chinese virtues, and this student at the Institute of Fine Arts in Beijing is very modestly turning his back on his model. In 1957 the director of the sculpture department, who had studied at the School of Fine Arts in Paris, still allowed the use of nude models.

99

In 1985 Hefei was witnessing the first effects of the politics of Openness: austerity and uniformity were being replaced by a shy kind of individualism which encouraged the affirmation of individual differences. And what better way to assert one's sense of individuality than to be photographed? 'I am photographed,' one might say, 'therefore I am.'

100

This photographer in Beijing in 1957 is using his old black box and wooden tripod. He is working a few hundred yards from the gates of the Forbidden City, which is painted – more vividly than life – on the backcloth he is using. The slogan 'Long Live the People's Republic of China' – which still looms above Tiananmen Square – will be all the clearer on this photograph, which will no doubt decorate the main family room for years to come.

101

Shenzhen, 1993: this enormous portrait of Deng Xiaoping (Teng Hsiao-ping) celebrates his famous speech on the politics of Openness, given here in Shenzhen in 1978. The portrait is cleaned on a regular basis using bamboo scaffolding – one of the splendid inventions of the Chinese genius.

102

At the entrance to a steelworks in the North East in 1957 a collection of photographs honours model workers, while those who have fallen from grace have had their names and photographs removed from the board. One cannot help wondering what has happened to these people since.

103

Shanghai, 1992: a few yards from the notices honouring the new managers others denounce a variety of crimes. Here a Shanghai workman is condemned to ten years in prison for having forced three young Shanghai girls into prostitution in Canton and pocketed the profits. Another criminal is condemned to twenty-five years' imprisonment for having stolen parts from the car factory where he was working, then for embezzling the proceeds from the sale of a gold ingot entrusted to him by his boss, and finally for committing bigamy. In the villages one often sees these kind of notices announcing death sentences – most frequently for rape and drug trafficking.

104

The right to divorce, provided for by the new Constitution of 1949, was very rarely granted during the sixties. Here, in 1965, a couple are requesting a

divorce in front of a handful of witnesses. The young woman gives as her reasons: 'My husband spends his salary on things outside the family. He beats our daughter. He isn't serious', while the husband claims: 'I don't love my wife any more. She is always criticizing me.' The judge recommends that they continue to try to live together.

105

Deng Xiaoping is seen here leaving his home to receive Georges Marchais, leader of the French Communist Party, during the latter's visit to Beijing in 1982. He is supported by his bodyguard, while his political secretary carries the present destined for Marchais. During lunch, which was held in the residence of one of China's last emperors, the Frenchman listened to Deng's description of the building's imperial origins and then commented: 'It must be sweet revenge for the Chinese Communists to be able to receive their guests in the splendid palaces that once belonged to China's emperors.' To which Deng simply replied: 'We are proud of our history.' The Zhong Shan jacket, which we see him wearing here, is still compulsory dress for the country's leaders. The four pockets symbolize the four Chinese virtues: politeness, honesty, fidelity and modesty.

106

In July 1971 Prime Minister Zhou Enlai (Chou En-lai) received a French delegation headed by Alain Peyrefitte. To the question 'During your stay in Paris, Prime Minister, did you learn French?' Zhou made a vehement gesture and replied emphatically: 'No! But I *did* learn, one, Marxism and, two, Leninism.' This meeting took place a few days after the announcement by Washington and Beijing of renewed diplomatic relations between the two countries – a spectacular reversal of alliances for which Zhou Enlai was primarily responsible. He is wearing the Mao badge above his left pocket.

107

This wide-open eye which stares unnervingly at the passers-by is simply an ophthalmologist's sign in Taiyuan, a provincial town – typical of so many in China – whose inhabitants are eager to show that they are keeping up with the times.

108

In Shenzhen in 1993 America is fashionable and American brands sell. In this advertisement for American ginseng the Statue of Liberty is brandishing the American flag and a bunch of ginseng roots. Chinese ginseng, which is grown in great quantities, is the best available, but an American brand has a greater chance of selling its tonic, fortifying and aphrodisiac qualities here. It is quite possible that neither the advertisers, nor the authorities, nor the passers-by recognize that this statue is a replica of the one erected as a symbol of Democracy by students in June 1989.

111

Tiananmen Square, at the entrance to the Forbidden City, 1993: this portrait of Mao is the only public one left in Beijing. Mao has been described as the son of a peasant who 'ploughed the century to change man' – to free him for ever from the constraints of money and profit, from inequalities and frivolous instincts. What are the fruits of Mao's efforts today? Where is the new man? Is this him, holding his girlfriend's hand, under Mao's steady gaze? This couple have all the attributes of today's 'nouveaux riches', all the new, flashy elements of the new ideal – plastic, fake leather, mini-skirt, dark glasses, sun hat …

112

Shenzhen, 1993: in a back street a poor man is lugging a pathetic bundle of belongings on his back, while above his head the Hong Kong actress Ye Yuqing, famous for her pornographic films (shown clandestinely in China), bares her breasts. Posters showing chubby-cheeked babies like this one are prized by expectant mothers, who believe that the more they look at such images the more beautiful their own baby will be.

113

Canton, 1993: a fashionable couple – he doing business on a portable phone, she playing with a Game Boy 'made in China'; in the meantime their lunch gets cold.

114

Jinan, capital of Shandong, 1993: this glimpse into the back room of a bakery demonstrates how exhausting piecework can be in trade and small businesses. No restrictions are imposed on the number of hours a person can work at a stretch.

115

A splendid McDonald's has opened a short bicycle ride away from Tiananmen Square, on the capital's most prestigious crossroads. McDonald's have been surprisingly successful with the Chinese, whose cuisine is one of the best in the world. Is this, one wonders, because of the exotic attraction of dishes that are beyond the scope of chopsticks? People who live in the provinces love having their photograph taken next to McDo the plastic clown – as this man is doing here in 1992 – just as they love having photographs taken under the portrait of Mao; and in the family album the two will rub shoulders – McDo and Mao …

116

A Chinese person would be able to tell immediately from the look of this young woman that this scene is in Shanghai. She is almost certainly a secretary and will be earning more than £300 a month if she is employed by a foreign firm and about £80 a month if the firm is Chinese. If a woman is attractive there are always ways in which she can supplement her income … The Taiwanese invest a great deal in China and have a soft spot for pretty Chinese girls.

117

Beijing, 1993: this rock group have a popular following in China's once austere capital. They have called themselves Tang, the name of the famous 6th-century dynasty – roughly the equivalent of a French group calling themselves Vercingetorix! Here, in this one-room council flat, they spend their time watching videos from Hong Kong and Taiwan, smoking Chinese tobacco and drinking green tea.

118-119

Canton, 1992: after a session of karaoke a hotel entertains its guests with a fashion parade, using all the latest technology: smoke-effects, fans, coloured lights and deafening music.

120

Beijing, 1992: in place of sixties denunciations of American imperialism and its lackeys this wall now carries the words 'The dream has become reality' above the image of a family laden with presents wrapped in the colours of the American flag. The couple are dressed in Western style and have a resolutely Western look. Only the little girl with her plaits looks Chinese, and she is there to promote the idea that having a daughter is fine, in a system where only one child per family is allowed. It is said today that in rural areas the desperation to conceive a son has led to the disappearance of millions of baby girls.

121

This young woman in Shenzhen is fashionably dressed in her blue jeans and blouse decorated with the American flag. Behind her a glass tower reflects a series of concrete towers and on the lower part of the tower a property company has displayed its telephone and fax numbers. In order to make up their budgets, ministers such as those for Education and Defence invest massive sums in luxury hotels, discotheques and information processing.

122

In Shanghai in 1993 the Bund is still the best place to watch the world go by. This man has probably come to Shanghai looking for work. Nearby a grandmother sits nursing a child on her knee. At the same spot in the early morning I have seen the numerous members of a tango club in action.

123

A little further along the Bund an elegant young mother, wearing skin-tight leggings and a jacket decorated with the outline of Shanghai's towers, is walking with her young son. Those Chinese children who have no siblings are fussed over and spoiled and tend as a result to be difficult and temperamental. The demographic limits imposed on Chinese families are particularly respected in the city and among members of the administration. What kind of future can this country expect when every leader is an only child?

124-125

In a little village in Shandong in 1993 this newspaper seller has hung up his fashion magazines from a line with clothes pegs (supposedly another Chinese invention). As more and more women take an interest in fashion, more and more women's magazines are printed – and the most remote rural areas are as much a part of this trend as the towns.

126

One certainly sees fewer beggars in China than in, say, France or England; more today, however, than in Mao's time, when they were not allowed to linger on the streets. Describing the Chinese beggars he saw in the thirties, Henri Michaux speaks of their 'spiritual, well-bred look, together with an impression of frail correctness such as one sometimes sees in old aristocratic families'. Behind this beggar, photographed in Shenzhen in 1993, a farmer has spread his maize harvest in the road, intending to sell it directly to the consumer.

127

Beijing, 1984: on the pavement, near Tiananmen Square, this officer has stopped to take out from its box his most recent purchase, a radio cassette player labelled *Made in China*, on which he will now be able to listen to the Chinese and Hong Kong hit parades. It may be something he has been dreaming of buying for some time; in any case it represents several months' pay.

128

Two young Shanghaians in high-heeled shoes return from a shopping spree in 1992.

129

Since the beginning of the 1990s fringe artists like this one have been living and working in an area to the west of Beijing. Their unorthodox, frequently hyperrealistic style has hindered them from showing their work in China, but their paintings sell for high prices in Hong Kong and Taiwan, and are also bought by foreign visitors.

130

The advertisement on the right extols the magnetic properties of a new mattress which produces mysterious effects on the body during sleep. The diagram shows which parts of the body are benefited by this method. On the footbridge, which spans one of Shenzhen's main avenues, a man with only one leg is lying in the rain on the wet ground and begging. In China physically and mentally handicapped people have traditionally been kept out of sight.

131

Alcatel's Shanghai-Bell factory in Shanghai, 1993: Belgian engineers point out how, thanks to their natural dexterity and intelligence, young workers like this one from China's rural areas adapt more quickly to such high-precision work than their Western counterparts.

132-133

During the fifties one still saw writers working in public in Beijing along with storytellers and puppeteers. This new public writer, seen here in 1993, has installed himself and his computer in the road in the midst of passing cars and bicycles. Computers are rapidly becoming part of everyday life in China – alongside the abacus, which remains resistant to change – and there is talk of new hotels where every room will have its own fax and computer.

134

Here in the south, in Shenzhen, advertising takes all shapes and forms. This beautiful sleeping woman is promoting the virtues of a rubber mat. The scene is inspired, I am told, by a famous painting in the Museum of the Revolution showing the death of a soldier on the battlefield during the Long March. One feels that Mao must be for ever turning in his grave… Since the politics of Openness advertising agencies, both large and small, have been springing up like mushrooms, drawing their inspiration from every available source.

135

Wangfujing is perhaps the street in Beijing which retains the best balance between Western fashions and Chinese identity, like the Chinese people themselves who, despite a taste for McDonalds and Coca-Cola, remain faithful to their country's traditions. The Chinese today seem to lead a double life, drawn, on the one hand, to the West and on the other still profoundly influenced by Chinese ways of thinking and acting.

136

In 1995 an old part of Shanghai was demolished to make way for the construction of a massive shopping complex covering a vast area. The building site and the equipment seem absurdly primitive. Under the falling rain odds and ends lie about – bits of string and wire.

137

This man had probably never seen a 'long nose' (the Chinese nickname for Westerners) until the day I photographed him, in April 1995. His astonished look told me that this mine in Taiyuan was no place for tourists – as the policemen, called by a handful of zealous Party members, were to emphasize (rather less politely). Some miners are very young, but all are proud of their work and the risks they face. According to *The People's Daily* there were more than 150 deaths in China's mines in 1994.

138-139

Before reaching towards the sky a tower-block under construction in Shenzhen must first be firmly anchored in the ground, since it needs to be both earthquake- and typhoon-proof. The technique is rudimentary: small motors protected by plastic sheets are used to lower the buckets of concrete into the circular wells from which the steel girders will rise. The architects and engineers are resident Chinese, the investors Chinese nationals living abroad: these men are China's 'Marshall Plan', and are largely responsible for the country's lightning economic surge.

140

It is not only Shanghai and Shenzhen but also the small provincial towns of three or four million inhabitants like Zhuzhou, Jinan and Shaoshan which are eager to show off their glass tower-blocks, their interchanges, their karaoke and … their pollution record. Here in Taiyuan, as in other towns, Chinese artisans are quick to adapt to new materials like these massive glass plates.

141

The people of Beijing have always liked eating in the street, summer and winter. With the end of Maoism small private restaurateurs like these were the first to return, to the general delight. Here, near Da Shala, in 1993, the smoke and the smell of delicious grilled brochettes have attracted a couple of local children. The Chinese are famous for their greed and Mao is quoted as saying: 'Why have a Revolution if the glazed duck is no better than before?'

142

In the vicinity of Shanghai in 1995 a few blocks of houses built in the last century are still standing, their walls covered with carefully repainted slogans.

143

This peasant told me how the inhabitants of this village, a hundred or so miles from Shanghai, each had to make a contribution so that the chief of police could build himself the finest house in the village. The house, seen in the background, is covered in glazed earthenware tiles in the style fashionable with the new 'parvenus'. The 'bathroom' style, as it is known, is directly imported from Taiwan and a must for the successful entrepreneur. The first indication of success is a tiled facade; three such walls point to a superior standing. Finally, if the owner has really succeeded – or if he is wily, like the chief of police here – all four walls will display a dazzling white sheen – and, simultaneously, the fortune of the occupants.

144-145

In Shenzhen in 1992, above a decidedly un-Chinese horizon of tower-blocks, Deng hovers in a sky reddened by the rising sun and proclaims the new religion: 'We must sustain socialism, the politics of openness and the improvement of living standards; otherwise we are finished.'

146

If it were not for the employees' bicycles, one might think this was Dallas or Houston. In 1992 the directors arrive at Shenzhen's Development Bank in air-conditioned Mercedes or Toyotas. The unskilled workers from far-flung corners of China, where all the houses are made of mud-brick, do not seem surprised by these futuristic towers. The Chinese are never surprised by anything.

147

Shanghai, 1993: cycle rickshaws, like this one, are used to transport a whole range of items, and there always seem to be children or people without a job ready to earn a few coppers by helping the cyclist to pull his load. In the background an advertisement for a Sino-American company is written in a boldly modernistic calligraphic style.

148

Shanghai, 1993: the Bund is being ripped apart by extensive construction work and pedestrians near the Semaphore are obliged to pick their way through an assault course.

149

Shanghai goes in for more extravagant advertising than anywhere else in China. Here it seems to have been quicker to hoist a Volkswagen Santana (the most popular foreign car) on to a roof than to put up a poster.

150-151

In Shenzhen in 1993 new tower-blocks spring up every month like mushrooms. The building methods are in striking contrast with the huge scale of the constructions.

152

Canton, 1992: the Chinese fascination with America is illustrated by T-shirts like this one, even if the wearer does not always understand the English slogans. It started in the south, most notably in Canton. The irony is that not so many years ago banners hung in this very place condemning America and the Americans.

153

This advertisement is for a private video club. Hong Kong is no great distance away and all kinds of cassettes enter the country illegally. Repressive measures are severe, particularly where pornography is concerned. Mao's portrait on the taxi windscreen is not a sign of political adherence: during a recent accident only the driver who had a picture of Mao in his vehicle emerged unscathed. The Chinese deduced from this that the Great Helmsman had entered the pantheon of protector gods and the fashion arose for putting Mao's portrait in windscreens, on keyrings and taximeters, etc., rather like a St Christopher.

154

In Shanghai in 1993, near the Stock Exchange, it is becoming inceasingly common to see a person using a portable telephone: given their natural business instinct, this is just the kind of gadget the Chinese like. A taxi driver or a sales assistant will be immediately able to tell you the precise exchange rate with the dollar.

155

Here in Taiyuan, the capital of Shanxi, this police officer is taking his family for a ride. (The motorbike and sidecar and the dark glasses are typical of the police.) In the background a car show-room has adopted a particularly eye-catching method for advertising its latest model by perching it on a roof.

156-157

Traffic jams, like this one in Shenzhen in 1993, are common, but no one blows their horn or loses their temper or shouts abuse. The Chinese are used to threading their way through crowds, whether on foot or on bicycles or, more recently, in cars.

158

Shenzhen, 1993: in the city's hairdressing quarter a number of salons are open late into the evening and even at night. The narrow streets are often lit with red and more especially yellow neon lighting.

159

Although the communists abolished the idea of 'masters', 'masters' chauffeurs' still exist in China, where they work not only for ministers and other officials, but also for the 'parvenus' so widely talked about today. The latter are proud of their luxury saloon car and their personal chauffeur, and prouder still of their registration number, which often includes four 8s (four times the symbol of fortune) and may have cost them as much as the Mercedes itself!

160

Dalian opened a stock exchange in 1994, but the deals are transacted in the street. These shareholders prefer not to show their faces. The one on the left is holding a share in a company that makes synthetic fibres and in order to show its value he is holding with it a 100-yuan note. (A hundred yuan is the average monthly wage of an unskilled worker.) The note features the likeness of four of the country's leaders, Mao, Zhou Enlai, Zhu De and Liu Shaoqi. The latter ended his life in a Maoist prison, but today the two men are 'reconciled' on the same banknote.

161

The women of Dalian – where the country's annual fashion fair takes place – are traditionally regarded as the most beautiful in China. This sophisticated young woman, photographed in 1994, is protecting her face from the sun – and unfortunately also from me.

162-163

Shenzhen, 1992: in this large amusement park each of China's provinces displays to foreigners and to its cousins in Hong Kong the natural beauties and architectural monuments (recreated in miniature) that are a source of its regional pride. On this wooden totem pole the sculptor has carved the Taoist symbol of yin and yang.

164

The Salem promotional umbrella serves to protect its user from the rain, but in the advertisement, painted on a wall in Shenzhen, gold coins rain down in response to a mere click of the fingers – on condition, of course, that one buys the recommended shares.

165

One wonders what is on this young boy's mind as he wanders through the crowd at a station in Shenzhen in 1994. Is he dreaming of money, that great god that is worshipped wherever he looks?

166

The Chinese have a surprising gift for mimicry. Imitating my gesture but without a camera, this young Shanghaian has already taken the mickey out of me before I have had time to take his picture.

My thanks to
Perrine Boudry, Thomas Consani, Patrice Fava, Eric Felices,
Nathalie des Gayets, Janine de Graverol, Stéphane Korb, Liu Jian,
Maud Moor, Nathalie Piquart, Elisabeth Pujol, Michèle Reby, Ondine Saglio,
Sun Gaofu, Patricia Tartour, Xiao Quan, and David and Alexis,
who gave of their best in helping to produce this book

and to all
the men, women and children (about 550) who appear in these pages,
and without whom this book would have been a sad affair

and finally
to Robert Delpire and Bertrand Eveno who were the first
to give this project their backing

M.R.

The photographs appearing
in this book and at the exhibition which it accompanied
were printed by Publimod Photo, Paris.
The majority of photographs reproduced here were taken
using Leica equipment and lenses.